THE STORY OF

JACKIE ROBINSON,
Bravest Man in Baseball

BY MARGARET DAVIDSON

ILLUSTRATED BY FLOYD COOPER

A YEARLING BOOK

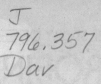

ABOUT THIS BOOK

The events described in this book are true. They have been carefully researched and excerpted from authentic autobiographies, writings, and commentaries. No part of this biography has been fictionalized.

To learn more about Jackie Robinson, ask your librarian to recommend other fine books you might read.

Especially for Leah Haber, with love

Published by
Bantam Doubleday Dell Books for Young Readers
a division of
Bantam Doubleday Dell Publishing Group, Inc.
1540 Broadway
New York, New York 10036

ISBN: 0-440-40019-8

Published by arrangement with Parachute Press, Inc.
Printed in the United States of America
January 1988

19   18   17

OPM

Contents

Dear Reader,

Jackie Robinson was a black pioneer. He broke the color barrier in major league baseball before the Civil Rights Movement—when open prejudice and outright racial slurs were much more common in the United States. Jackie Robinson was often called ugly names such as burr-head, coon, jungle-bunny, and nigger. Some of these words—ones not usually found in books for children—are in this book because they were such a real and painful part of Jackie Robinson's life.

Jackie Robinson was a brave, tough, caring man who wouldn't let name-calling stop him. Although his fight for equality took place on the baseball diamond, his "wins" have helped to better the lives of people everywhere.

Margaret Davidson

Before It All Began

THIS IS JACKIE ROBINSON'S STORY. BUT IT really begins fifteen years before he was born. It begins with a young man named Branch Rickey.

Branch Rickey coached a college baseball team in Ohio. One spring day in 1904 he took his boys out of town to play another college in South Bend, Indiana. So they had to stay the night at a hotel. The college boys joked and laughed as they signed their names in the hotel register. The hotel clerk was smiling, too. But then Charlie Thomas started to sign. And suddenly the clerk wasn't smiling anymore.

"No niggers allowed!" he snapped as he jerked the register away from Charlie.

"You don't understand," Branch Rickey said. "Charlie is part of my team, and—"

"I don't care who he is," the clerk interrupted angrily. "We don't register colored in this hotel."

"Now, listen here," Branch Rickey said, beginning to get angry, too. "We're here to play your town's university. We are their guests, and we're not going to put up with this kind of treatment!"

"Mr. Rickey," Charlie Thomas said softly, "I don't want to cause any trouble for you or the team. Maybe I'd better just go home."

"No!" said Rickey. "We have to find some way out of this." He turned to the clerk. "Would you object if Charlie slept in an extra bed in my room? Then you wouldn't have to register him."

The clerk wasn't happy about it. But finally he muttered, "Oh, all right. I guess you can do that."

A few minutes later Rickey went up to his room. And he never forgot what he saw when he opened the door.

Charlie was sitting on the edge of a chair, sobbing. "It's my skin, isn't it?" he said. "If I could just tear it off, then I'd be like everyone else. It's my skin, Mr. Rickey."

Then he held up his hands and said, "If only they were white, I'd be treated as good as anybody, wouldn't I, Mr. Rickey?"

Branch Rickey's answer seemed to come from somewhere very deep inside himself. "Charlie, I promise you this. The day will come when they won't have to be white."

It was a promise Branch Rickey never forgot.

Pro at an Early Age

IT WAS TOWARD THE END OF A FINE FALL day on Pepper Street in Pasadena, California. Mallie Robinson had just called her children in to dinner. The first to arrive was six-year-old Jackie. "Mama, Mama, guess what?" he cried as he came skidding into the kitchen.

Mallie smiled at her youngest son. He was always bursting with some kind of hard-to-hold-in news. Now Jackie puffed out his chest and announced, "You don't have to fix lunch for me to take to school tomorrow. Or ever again!"

Mallie laughed. All five of her children had big appetites. But Jackie's was a family joke—everyone said he ate like a horse. "So what are you going to do?" she asked, still chuckling. "Go on a diet?"

"No, ma'am! We've got two softball teams at school. And the kids on one of them say

4

they'll split their lunches with me if I promise to play on their side!"

"You might say," Jackie Robinson wrote many years later, "that I turned professional at an early age."

All the young Robinsons were natural athletes. Jackie's oldest brother, Edgar, could do all sorts of fancy tricks on his roller skates. Frank, the next oldest, was a sprinter. Mack was also a runner, but he spent more time working on his broad jump. And Willa Mae, Jackie's only sister, was good at any sport girls were allowed to play in the 1920s.

But right from the beginning it was plain that Jackie was going to be different. He wasn't just a fine athlete. He was, as a friend said, "one of a kind."

Baseball, football, relay racing, dodgeball, swimming—there didn't seem to be a sport he wasn't good at. He also had the ability to concentrate, something that all great athletes must have. Another of his playmates remembered a summer when all the youngsters in the neighborhood were busy playing marbles. "We'd get up and play from morning until night. But the rest of us would sometimes wander off. Not Jackie. He'd just keep on practicing—and getting better and better."

This friend also remembered that Jackie was usually the leader of any street game they played. "And because he was so good, he'd always pick the younger kids, the kids with less ability, to play on his team. Even then he'd figure out a way to beat the other team. He always figured things out so that we'd all get a chance to play, to compete, and have a good time."

Whatever the game he was playing, Jackie was always eager to go home at the end of the day. Home for the Robinsons was a small, shabby house in a run-down section of Pasadena, California. But Jackie didn't care what the house looked like, for it contained the one thing that mattered most of all— love.

The heart of the Robinson house was Jackie's mother, Mallie. "She was wise in the ways of human beings," Jackie said later. "And I thought she must have some kind of magic to do all the things she did, to work so hard, and never complain, and make us all feel happy." Jackie's brother Mack agreed. "She had a way of saying and doing things that brought out the best in all of us."

Mallie Robinson worked long and hard every day to support her family. But no matter how tired she was, she always had time in the evening to listen to what they had done that day. Time to talk about any plans or feelings or worries they might want to share.

What Jackie liked best, though, were the times she talked about the past. Sometimes she spoke about her father, who had been a slave when he was Jackie's age. Jackie tried hard to imagine what it must have felt like to be owned like a dog or a horse. But he couldn't. Young as he was, he was already too strong-willed to picture being bossed around by someone else.

Mallie spoke of the days when she had been growing up, and how desperately poor her family had been. But they'd still been happy because they had had the one thing that was really important.

"What's that, Mama?" Jackie would say, his eyes shining because he already knew.

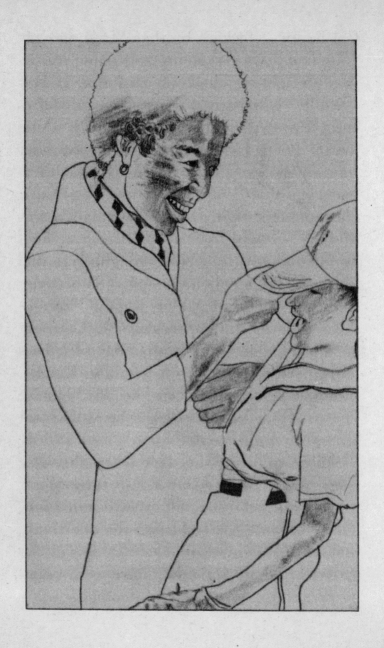

"Pride," Mrs. Robinson would answer. "Pride in ourselves."

Jackie's favorite story was about the day he'd been born in a tumbledown cabin in the red clay country of rural Georgia.

It had been cold and stormy that last day of January, 1919, and an icy wind was whistling through the cracks in the walls. Mallie watched from bed with Jackie in her arms as her husband, Jerry, tried to fix the baby's first meal. He was mixing sugar and melted lard together and struggling to stuff this mixture into a small piece of cheesecloth for Jackie to suck on. He was doing his best, but he was clumsy, and quite a lot of it was landing on the floor.

"What did you do then, Mama?" Jackie would always ask when she came to this part of the story.

"Why, I bent and kissed you," Mallie Robinson would answer. "And then I said, 'Bless you, boy. For you to survive all this, God will *have* to keep His eye on you.'"

Mallie's eyes always twinkled when she thought of that day. But then often afterward she'd grow silent and sad. And Jackie would know she was thinking of the bad time right after that. The time his father went away.

Jerry Robinson had been a sharecropper. The land he farmed and the shack his family lived in belonged to someone else—a white farmer named Sasser. Jerry worked very hard. But Mr. Sasser paid him almost nothing in return. There was no way he could save money to buy land and a home of his own, and this made him very restless.

When Jackie was a baby, Jerry Robinson told his wife he couldn't stand this going-nowhere life any longer. He had decided to visit a brother in Texas. He'd hunt for a better job there—a job with some sort of future—and then he promised to send for his family.

But that was a promise Jerry Robinson did not keep. Mallie never heard from him again. Suddenly she was the head of the Robinson family.

Mallie rarely talked about that day when she watched her husband walk out of their lives. But she did tell Jackie about something that happened not long afterward. She and the children were still in the cabin on Mr. Sasser's land. One morning a very angry Mr. Sasser came by. "Why didn't you warn me that Jerry was planning to leave?" he yelled. "Then I could have got the sheriff to stop him!"

Mallie was a small woman. But whenever she got to this part of the story, she would draw herself up until she seemed very tall. "But slavery's *over*, Mr. Sasser," she had answered on that day long ago. "And that man is *free* to go where he pleases."

Oh, how Jackie loved that story! One day, when he was grown, Jackie Robinson would be called a pioneer—a man who dared to fight "the way things were." But Jackie always said that it was his mother who had shown him how to be brave.

It took all of Mallie's courage to do what she did next. Life was not good for Negroes in Georgia as the 1920s were about to begin. Almost everything was segregated. Blacks and whites led separate lives in almost every way. Negroes lived in the most run-down houses. They could only get the hard, dirty, dangerous jobs that no one else wanted. And they were paid far less money than whites.

Even children suffered from segregation. Black boys and girls had to go to separate schools. And these schools were almost always crowded, poorly equipped, and run-down.

One day Mallie got a letter from her brother Burton, who lived in California. There, he said, the education was not segregated. Both black and white children went to the same schools.

That really excited Mallie, for she had a dream for her five children. She'd never had much of an education herself. But she wanted this next generation of Robinsons to go to good schools and learn more than she had. She even dreamed that they might one day go to college.

Mallie had the courage to act on her dream. In the spring of 1920, when Jackie was only sixteen months old, she left her relatives and friends and everything she knew and took her family to California. "That was my mother," Jackie Robinson wrote. "She was the real trailblazer in the family."

Jackie was content with much of his life in California. School was easy for him. He had many friends and a close and loving family. "Jackie was a happy-go-lucky kid," one of those friends remembered. "A lot of fun. He always had some trick up his sleeve." As Jackie grew older, though, two things began to bother him.

One was poverty. Mallie Robinson worked as a maid. Every morning before dawn she left home to wash and iron and cook and clean in other people's houses. The money she received for all this work was barely enough to feed her family.

What Jackie remembered most about those days was food, mainly the lack of it. "Sometimes there were only two meals a day," he wrote later. He remembered racing home after school to find only stale bread and sugar in the house. Then he'd sweeten a glass of water with the sugar, munch on a piece of bread, and pretend he was eating steak and drinking strawberry soda pop. The only trouble was, his stomach never believed him. "And some days," Jackie continued,

13

"we wouldn't have eaten at all if it hadn't been for the leftovers my mother was able to bring home from her job."

But what made Jackie unhappiest of all was prejudice. Although life in California wasn't nearly as segregated as it was in the South, there were many prejudiced people around—people who simply couldn't accept anyone with a darker skin as an equal.

Jackie never forgot something that happened to him when he was only eight years old. He was sweeping the walk in front of his house when a white girl about his age came out of her house across the street. "Nigger, nigger, nigger boy!" she began to chant.

Jackie's older brother, Edgar, who could remember living in Georgia, had told him that the worst thing you could call a white person there was "cracker."

So Jackie began to chant in return, "Cracker, cracker, cracker girl!"

The little girl came back with, "Cracker's good to eat. Nigger's only good to beat!"

Before Jackie could think of anything to top *that,* the girl's father came storming out of the house. He, too, started to yell at

Jackie. Then he picked up a handful of small rocks and began to fling them at him.

Jackie Robinson would always hate to run from trouble. He didn't run from it now. He just scooped up some rocks of his own and began hurling them back.

The fight didn't last long. The girl's mother ran out and made her husband stop. "Imagine," she scolded, "throwing rocks at a mere child!"

Jackie wasn't hurt. Not physically, at least. But he never forgot how painful it was to know that someone—a person who didn't even know him—could dislike him so much.

Later he learned that almost all black children repeatedly suffered experiences like this. He also learned that, all too often, they began believing the terrible messages they were getting. Messages that said "You're no good." "You can't make it." And "Why even try?" Little by little they'd be filled with what the civil rights leader Martin Luther King, Jr., would one day call "a sense of no-bodyness."

Jackie didn't react this way. Instead, he became angry. The way he expressed his anger was to join a gang. The Pepper Street Gang was made up of Negroes, Japanese, and Mexicans. The boys had a lot of free time on their hands—time to find ways of getting into trouble.

A favorite pastime was to steal balls from a nearby golf course. Jackie and the others would hide behind some bushes and wait until a golfer sent a ball sailing over a nearby hill. When this happened someone, usually Jackie, because he was so fast, would dash out and grab the ball. Then they'd all watch, giggling, as the puzzled golfer came into view, scratching his head and hunting for his ball. When he'd given up and moved on, they'd take the ball back to the club-house and sell it to somebody else.

The gang also swiped fruit from nearby stores. Another popular way to pass the time was to perch on a curb and throw clods of dirt at passing cars. Jackie usually hit the most, because his aim was so good.

No wonder Jackie and the other members of the Pepper Street Gang were often hauled down to the local police station. There a policeman named Captain Morgan would give them stern lectures about the awful things that lay in wait for them if they didn't shape up.

Jackie was bawled out more than the others, not because of what he'd been doing, but because he couldn't seem to keep his mouth shut. Mallie Robinson had taught her children to be polite. But she'd also taught them to stand up for their rights. She'd taught them to be unafraid, too. So when Jackie thought the policeman was being unfair, he said so.

This didn't make Captain Morgan happy at all. "You know, Robinson, you're a real pop-off!" he'd shout. "That mouth of yours is going to get you in big trouble one day!"

Captain Morgan's dire predictions did come true for a few of the boys. They grew up to commit serious crimes. Jackie said he might have, too, except for one man.

Carl Anderson worked at a shop across the street from where the Pepper Street Gang spent most of their time. One day he took Jackie aside. He said he'd watched the boy stealing fruit and throwing dirt at cars. He knew it wasn't much—yet. But if Jackie went on like that, he'd land in real trouble.

What Jackie had to admit to himself, Carl Anderson continued, was that he didn't really belong in a gang. He was simply following the crowd because he was afraid to be thought different.

Jackie could only hang his head in shame, because he knew Mr. Anderson was right. But what really made Jackie decide to quit the gang were Carl Anderson's final words. "I know your mother and she's a fine woman," he said softly. "How do you think she'd feel if one day she had to watch you being taken off to jail?"

"Stop Robinson!"

JACKIE DROPPED OUT OF THE PEPPER Street Gang. What took its place—what helped him keep his balance during those difficult growing-up years—were sports. Participating in sports gave him a feeling of accomplishment, a feeling of doing something well. Sports also provided him with a way to burn off some of his anger about being black in a mainly white society.

There didn't seem to be anything he couldn't do. By the time Jackie got to Muir Technical High School, he was a star athlete in baseball, football, basketball, and track. Jackie's fierce will to win helped the rest of his teammates play like demons, too. Soon the coaches of opposing teams were giving their players just one instruction: "Stop Robinson!"

One of the opposing players said later that they tried calling him all sorts of names, hoping to get him so mad he'd lose his concentration. "But we soon found out that the madder you made him, the better he played. He was interested in winning, not in anything else."

For years Jackie had seen his mother working almost constantly. After he graduated from high school, he wanted to find a full-time job so he could bring home money to her. But Mallie Robinson wouldn't hear of it. She had always dreamed of sending her children to college, and so she convinced Jackie to go. In the fall of 1937 Jackie entered Pasadena Junior College.

Before Jackie arrived at the college, sports fans weren't interested in the school teams. But soon they began to hear about "a kid out there who's doing some pretty amazing things."

Amazing is one thing. Impossible is another. One spring day during Jackie's freshman year that's what he seemed to face, an impossible choice. Two important sports events were being held the same Saturday afternoon, and Jackie wanted to be in both of them.

One was a track meet in Pomona. The

other was a championship baseball game in Glendale. The two towns were more than forty miles apart. "So you'll just have to pick one or the other," his coach told him. "You can't be in two places at once."

But Jackie thought up a scheme that just might do it—if everything went like clockwork. He asked the officials of the track meet if he could be the first to do the broad jump. That was the event he was competing in. And they said he could.

People who know sports speak of something called *desire*. It's a great surge of emotional energy that helps an athlete do fantastic things. Jackie certainly had desire that day. He crouched . . . He tensed . . . He pounded down the track to the take-off board . . .

When he landed, the officials said he'd jumped twenty-three feet, six inches. They also said he might as well stop right there, even though he had the right to try twice more. Nobody else was going to top that jump.

But Jackie wasn't just competing against other athletes that day. He was also competing against himself. So once more he crouched—and tensed—and pounded down the track. This time he landed a full foot farther than before.

Surely *now* he'd be content. But no. The desire still burned in him. For the third time he jumped . . . and went still another foot more! *Twenty-five feet, six and a half inches.* Jackie Robinson had set a new junior college world record.

But he had no time to think about that now. Already his mind was on the game in Glendale. As a friend's car raced him over California's winding roads, Jackie wriggled out of his track suit and into his baseball uniform.

"Hurry," he kept urging, for he knew the game had already started. Jackie arrived in the third inning and Pasadena was in trouble. By fielding and hitting and running, Jackie helped turn the game around and spark his team to a 5–3 victory, making them junior college champions of Southern California.

By Jackie's second year crowds gathered wherever he played. Newspaper writers started to invent names for him like "The Dusky Flash," and "The Midnight Express."

Pasadena Junior College was a two-year school. But that didn't mean Jackie's college sports career was over when he graduated. By now his name was known up and down the West Coast. And the coaches of major universities wanted him on their teams.

One after another they came to the little house on Pepper Street to offer Jackie tempting athletic scholarships—a way of paying his college expenses. The strangest offer came from the coach of a big college in northern California. He wanted Jackie to play for him. But if Jackie decided not to, the coach was willing to arrange a scholarship to some *eastern* college. What he meant was, if Jackie wouldn't play for his school, he wanted him far, far away—where he wouldn't be playing against it.

Jackie finally decided to go to the University of California at Los Angeles. At UCLA, as it is called, Jackie continued his seemingly endless list of sports triumphs.

Usually a college athlete chose one sport he or she was especially good at and special-ized in that. But Jackie wanted it all. First he played halfback on the football team, and as usual, he played brilliantly. "You'd have to have a row of tanks to stop this guy Robinson," an opposing coach grumbled.

Then Jackie went out for basketball, and the story was the same. "I say he's the best basketball player in college sports," another coach commented.

After basketball season was over he turned to track and baseball. And he excelled at them, too. When honors were awarded at the end of the year, Jackie became the first student in UCLA history to win a letter in all four sports.

He repeated this performance in his second year. By now many people were saying that Jackie's athletic career was "the stuff of storybooks." Sportswriters were falling over one another trying to find ways to express how they felt about his talent.

"Best all-around athlete ever to play on the West Coast."

"The thought of another athlete such as Jack Robinson appearing upon the scene seems utterly fantastic."

"The best Negro athlete of all time."

"The best all-around athlete in America."

"There may have been better football players, better basketball players, better baseball players, and better track men, but worry my memory as I will, I can think of nobody more able in the four put together."

And it wasn't only sportswriters who thought he was "one of a kind." Jimmy Dykes, manager of the Chicago White Sox, a professional baseball team, happened to see Jackie play one day. "I'd hire that boy to play major league ball at a moment's notice—if only he were white," he said.

That was the problem Jackie faced now that his college days had come to an end. He wanted to continue as an athlete. But where? All professional team sports—baseball, football, and basketball—were closed to blacks.

As things turned out, this was a problem Jackie wouldn't have to worry about for the next few years. For, in 1941, history stepped in and offered him a job he couldn't refuse. The United States Army wanted him as a soldier in World War II.

Lieutenant Robinson

PRIVATE JACKIE ROBINSON WAS SENT TO Fort Riley, Kansas, for his basic training. And it was here, he wrote later, that he first met Jim Crow. Jim Crow was a system, "a really rigid pattern of discrimination that kept Negroes down in as many ways as possible."

When Jackie finished basic training, he applied for Officers Candidate School, or OCS, which trained men to become officers. But after Jackie applied, he was met by a baffling silence. Finally someone told him to wise up.

By law Negroes could be officers, but that didn't mean anything at Fort Riley. Here there was a policy—a kind of hidden understanding—that blacks would never be given the chance. It was the system, the way things were. Whenever a Negro applied, he was always rejected with the same stock phrase, "He is not a leader of men."

27

Well, system or not, Jackie was ready as usual to fight for what he thought was right. Luckily for him he had a powerful friend. Joe Louis, the heavyweight boxing champion of the world, was in the army, too. And he was black. What's more, he'd just been sent to Fort Riley.

Jackie told Louis that the Jim Crow system was making it impossible for him and other Negroes to get into Officers Candidate School. Joe Louis said he'd try to help. Joe Louis was the most famous Negro in America, and he had a great deal of influence. He contacted a high government official in Washington, D.C. A few days later the official came to investigate. Wheels began to turn. And before long Jim Crow had to back down a little. Jackie and several other black soldiers were accepted into OCS.

On graduation Jackie became Lieutenant Robinson and was appointed morale officer of a Negro company. An important part of his job was to make life as pleasant as possible for his men.

Jackie soon found there was a real need for that. One day he heard some of the soldiers talking about the way they were being treated at the Post Exchange. The PX, as it was called, was a military store and a restaurant and a meeting place for friends. But most of its services were segregated, including the restaurant. And very few tables were set aside for black troops. This meant that they often had to stand in long lines, even when "white only" tables were empty.

One GI complained bitterly that the army planned to send him ten thousand miles away to fight for democracy, but only a few hundred feet away he wasn't free to sit on a chair and drink a bottle of beer.

"Yeah," another muttered. "I say it's stupid to think you can treat a man like a packhorse and then have him get in a feverish rage to die for his country."

Just then they noticed Jackie standing there.

"Well, well," one of the soldiers drawled. "If it isn't the company morale officer. Lieutenant, I ask you. What are you gonna do? The morale is *low*!"

"I'll tell you what I'm going to do, Corporal," Jackie answered. "I'm going to see what can be done to change the situation at the PX."

"Yeah . . ."

"Sure . . ."

"Best of luck, Lieutenant . . ."

It was plain that his men didn't believe he stood a chance of changing anything. Jackie wasn't sure he did either. But he was certainly going to try.

As soon as Jackie got to his office, he telephoned the provost marshal, the major in charge of the PX. At first he was very proper. He identified himself as Lieutenant Robinson. Then he asked, "Sir, is there an official policy of segregation at the Post Exchange? Or is it just custom?"

The major was equally polite. "Lieutenant, I guess you could say it's both custom and policy."

At this Jackie's voice became a little more crisp. "Well, my men protest this setup where white troops can come in and get service without delay, but Negro troops have to stand in lines even to buy a bottle of Coke or a candy bar."

"Lieutenant, we're doing the best we can

to provide service to our colored troops," the major answered. "But I think you can understand we can't start taking things away from whites and giving them to colored soldiers . . ."

"Why not?" Jackie's voice was dangerously soft, for he was beginning to suspect something. Could it be that the provost marshal didn't know *he* was black, too?

"Why, it would cause a real problem. It might adversely affect the morale of our white troops."

"What do you think it's doing to the morale of the Negro troops?" Jackie said more loudly. "I'm their morale officer, and I've heard them griping about this Jim Crow setup. You've got fellows here preparing to go abroad and defend their country just like anybody else!"

The major began to lose patience. "Lieutenant," he snapped. "Are you suggesting that we ought to *mix* the races at the Post Exchange? Let these Negro troops sit where they please?"

"That's exactly what I'm suggesting," Jackie shot back. "When they get over into those battle areas, nobody's going to separate any bullets and label them 'for white troops' and 'for colored troops.' "

"Now, be reasonable, Lieutenant Robinson," the major answered coldly. "Let me put it this way. How would you like to have your wife sitting next to a nigger?"

For one stunned moment Jackie stared at the telephone in his hand. Then he forgot that you were always polite to a superior officer in the army. He forgot everything except the wild rage that was surging through him.

"Major," he shouted, "I happen to *be* a Negro, and I don't know that having someone's wife sitting next to a Negro is any worse than having her sit next to some of the white soldiers I've seen around here!"

"Now, you listen to me—"

But Jackie was a long way past listening. "It's obvious to me that guys who think like you are the reason why conditions are so bad in this camp," he thundered. "You're the kind of guy who has no conception of what democracy is all about, and what's more, you've got no business enjoying it!"

There was a sharp *click*. And Jackie realized he was shouting into an empty line. The provost marshal had hung up.

The minute Jackie stopped yelling he realized how quiet the office was. "It was silent as a tomb," he said later. "Not even a typewriter was moving." Jackie knew he could be in big trouble for talking that way to a higher-ranking officer. But he was still so furious he didn't care.

A few minutes later he strode into the office of his battalion commander, Colonel Longley. "Uh, sir, I've just had a somewhat lively discussion with the provost marshal . . ." he began, standing at rigid attention.

"You don't need to tell me," Colonel Longley replied dryly. "I heard it. So did everyone else." Then he smiled just a little and motioned Jackie to sit down. "Why don't you tell me what this is all about?"

The colonel listened carefully. Then he said, "I don't like this segregated setup any better than you do, Robinson. I don't think it's good for my battalion *or* for my country." And he promised to write the commanding general of Fort Riley to see what could be done about the PX.

Jackie was happy that the white colonel cared enough to do that. But he wasn't hopeful that much would happen. He was right. A few more tables were set aside for Negro soldiers. But the basic policy of segregation remained firmly in place.

Not long after that Jackie tangled in an even more personal—and painful—way with Jim Crow. Fort Riley had an exceptional baseball team. Naturally Jackie wanted to play with them, so he went out for a practice session.

One of the players on that team was Pete Reiser. Reiser had played with the major league Brooklyn Dodgers before the war, and would again once the war was over. Later he wrote about that day.

"We were practicing when a Negro lieutenant came out for the team," he remembered. "But the coach told him, 'You have to play with the colored team.' That was a sick joke. There *was* no colored team. The black lieutenant didn't speak. He just stood there for a while, watched us work out, then he turned and walked away. I didn't know his name then, but that was the first time I saw

35

Jackie Robinson. I can still see him slowly walking away."

It was no wonder that with experiences like these, Jackie was not sorry when his days as Lieutenant Robinson came to an end.

But what was ordinary citizen Mr. Robinson going to do now? After a while he decided to take a job with the Kansas City Monarchs, an all-Negro baseball team.

As usual he had a wonderful time playing ball, but off the field his thoughts were often gloomy. His wages were low, and he could hope for little more, no matter how long he played. Living conditions were also bad. When the team traveled, they often had to sleep on the bus because no white hotel would have them. Many times they'd have to eat on the bus, too, because even the most run-down white lunch counter would refuse them service.

Jackie was also lonely. He was engaged to be married to a beautiful young woman named Rachel Isum, or Rae as he called her. Rae was back in California, though, so he didn't see her for months at a time.

But his gloomiest thoughts were about his future. When he was in college, sportswriters had said he was "the most promising athlete in America." Those days as a superstar athlete were ancient history, however. Now he was twenty-six years old. That was no longer young for an athlete. And what did he have to look forward to? Playing segregated baseball for a team most of America had never heard of?

Later Jackie Robinson said that was the worst time he could remember. He didn't know that his life was about to take an amazing turn—because of an amazing man named Branch Rickey.

A Special Kind of Guts

BRANCH RICKEY WAS GENERAL MANAGER of the Brooklyn Dodgers baseball team. He had held this and other important positions in major league baseball for more than thirty years. During that time he'd come to be called "The Brain" because he did his job so well. "He could spot things in a man that nobody else could," one of his players said.

Branch Rickey was more than smart, though. He was also a deeply caring man who had never forgotten something that had happened more than forty years before.

He remembered when he'd been a young coach of a college baseball team. He remembered taking that team to another town and trying to register at a hotel. He remembered the clerk saying, "No niggers allowed." He remembered the young Negro ballplayer Charlie Thomas holding up his hands and saying, "It's my hands, isn't it, Mr. Rickey? If only they were white, I'd be treated as good as anybody, wouldn't I?"

And Rickey never forgot his answer to Charlie's agonized question. He had promised that one day it wouldn't matter what color they were.

Branch Rickey was older and wiser now. He knew that the color of a person's skin still mattered in too many ways and too many places. And he knew he couldn't change the whole unjust world. Well, he wasn't planning to. He was planning to take on only one part of it—professional baseball.

In 1945 there were six teams in the National League and six in the American—all of them entirely white. Now Branch Rickey planned to put a black player on his Brooklyn Dodgers.

He knew, of course, that this would make a lot of people very angry. Some would be so angry they'd try to stop him any way they could. So at first he kept his plan a deep secret.

He sent his scouts out to hunt for the best black ballplayer they could find, but he didn't tell them the real reason for this search. He said he was planning to start a new Negro team called the Brooklyn Brown Dodgers.

Rickey wanted his scouts to search for outstanding athletic ability. He also wanted them to gather information about the man's character and the way he lived, because, as he said, "I needed a young man who could keep performing while under great pressure and abuse. I needed a man with spirit who also had the self-control to avoid reacting to his tormentors. I needed a man who led a clean life off the field, because everyone would be trying to find something wrong he'd done. There just weren't very many such humans."

One by one the scouts' reports began to come in. Several names were mentioned more than once. But the name that came up again and again was Jack Roosevelt Robinson. His athletic skills were almost legendary. He was also clean-living and "didn't run around with girls," as one of the reports noted. The only negative thing the scouts turned up was that Jackie had a way of "arguing with white folks."

This didn't bother Rickey a bit. "I'd say

Robinson's biggest crime was being born a Negro," he said to a friend one day. "If he'd been a white player, he would have been praised to the skies as a fighter, a real competitor, a ballplayer's ballplayer. Well, I need a player now with some aggressiveness, because he's got to be bold and gritty enough to stand up unflinchingly to what I'm sure will come."

In August of 1945 Branch Rickey sent Clyde Sukeforth, his head scout, to bring Jackie Robinson back to the Brooklyn Dodger office in New York City. It was time for the two men who would change baseball forever to meet face-to-face.

"So you're Jackie Robinson. I've heard some mighty fine things about you," Rickey said as Jackie came into his office.

Then he got right down to business. "Do you know why you're here today?"

"I've heard rumors that you're starting a new Negro team called . . ," Jackie began. But he stopped when he saw that Branch Rickey was shaking his head.

"No, that isn't it. Jackie, you were brought here today to talk about playing for the Brooklyn organization itself."

Play for the Dodgers? Jackie said later that his reaction to this news was "like some kind of weird emotional mixture churning in a blender." He was thrilled, scared, excited, and amazed. Most of all he was speechless. Which was just as well. Branch Rickey was a man of many words.

"Tell me, Jackie," he said, waving a big, fat cigar in the air. "What would you do if you were standing in the batter's box and the pitcher sent a fast ball straight at your head. A ball that sends you right on your backside?"

What was the man getting at? Jackie wondered. But he answered quietly, "I've been thrown at before, Mr. Rickey. I'd just pick myself up and go on playing ball."

Rickey kept on probing. "What would you do if you were playing second base and another player came down from first? What would you do if he came flying in with his spikes high, cutting you on the leg? What would you do if he laughed as the blood ran down your leg and said, 'That'll teach you, nigger!'?"

Jackie sensed that Mr. Rickey wanted him to say he'd just meekly take things like that. But how could he? And *why* should he? All his life he'd been fighting to show the world that Negroes were not cowards, were not inferiors. So he snapped, "Mr. Rickey, what do you want? A Negro ballplayer who is *afraid* to fight back?"

This was just what Branch Rickey had been waiting for. "No!" he roared. "What I want is a ballplayer with guts enough *not* to fight back!"

The Dodger manager sat back. Then he went on in a quieter voice, "It's like this, Jackie. We've got virtually nobody on our side. No owners, no umpires, very few players or newspapermen. I'm afraid a great many fans will be hostile, too. No, we can win only if we can convince the world that I'm doing this because you're a great ballplayer and a fine gentleman."

Jackie leaned forward, his hands locked tightly together. "Mr. Rickey, you make this sound like some kind of a battle."

"That's exactly what it is!" Once more Rickey used his cigar to punctuate his

words. "I know you're strong-willed, Jackie. And I admire that in you. I like a fight as well as you do. But this is a battle we won't be able to fight our way through. Not with our fists." Rickey continued by describing an opposing player sliding into Jackie and calling him a string of foul names. "I wouldn't blame you if you came up swinging. You'd be right. You'd be justified. But you'd also set the cause back twenty years. So at first our weapons will have to be your base hits and daring plays . . ."

Branch Rickey paused for a moment. Then he added, "And your pride, Jackie— your swallowed pride."

"I think I understand," Jackie said in a low voice.

But Rickey wasn't satisfied with these words. He wanted Jackie to do more than *think* he understood. He wanted him to really *feel* what it was going to be like to be the first black man in baseball.

So, pacing up and down, he continued acting out scenes Jackie would have to be prepared for. He became a hotel clerk telling Jackie that "colored can't sleep in this hotel." He was a restaurant owner saying that Jackie would have to eat in the kitchen. He acted out an umpire calling him one ugly racial name after another.

Finally Rickey sank back in his chair again. "So I must ask you again," he said, mopping his face with his handkerchief, "have you got the guts to play the game no matter what happens?"

Jackie didn't answer right away, not now that he really understood what lay ahead of him. But finally he nodded. "I can do it," he answered. "I can turn the other cheek for a while. If you take this gamble, I promise you there will be no incidents."

Finally Branch Rickey knew he could relax. He'd found the right man. A man strong enough *not* to lose his temper. Now he leaned forward and put his hand on Jackie's shoulder. "Son, I'm sorry I had to be so rough on you. But you're a pioneer. You'll be carrying the reputation of a whole race on your shoulders. And if you bear it well, the day will come when every team in baseball will open their doors to Negroes."

The Noble Experiment

ALL TOO SOON JACKIE FOUND OUT THAT Branch Rickey was right. Almost nobody was on their side.

In October of 1945 the Dodger manager released a short statement to the press, saying that Jackie Robinson had been signed to the Montreal Royals. The Royals were the top Dodger farm team, where young players got experience before moving up to the major leagues. Now everyone knew what Rickey planned to do—bring Jackie into the Brooklyn Dodgers itself.

Rickey called this the "noble experiment." Reaction to it was quick, and almost all negative. People said it wouldn't work because Negroes lacked "the desire" to play the game. They told Rickey that blacks weren't in major league baseball because as a race, they weren't bright or talented enough. Everyone knew, they said, that blacks couldn't handle pressure situations.

"That is why there's not a single Negro player with major league possibilities," wrote *Sporting News,* the bible of the entire sports world.

Clay Hopper, the manager of the Montreal Royals, was also upset by the news. "Don't do this to me, Mr. Rickey," he begged. "I'm from Mississippi, and I'll never be able to explain it to the folks back home."

Rickey refused to change his mind. "You'll see, Clay," he said, "Jackie Robinson has some superhuman skills."

"But that's just it," Clay Hopper answered in a troubled voice. "Do you really believe a nigger is a human being?"

Later Branch Rickey said that for a moment he was very angry. Then he realized that Hopper was simply voicing something he'd been taught almost from birth—that Negroes were subhuman. So he answered quietly, "Forget about what color he is, Clay. Your job is to see that he plays as well as possible, and nothing else."

Luckily not every reaction was so negative. One sportswriter reminded his readers that the Second World War had just ended.

"Those who were good enough to fight and die by the side of whites are plenty good enough to play by the side of whites," he wrote.

Rudy York, a great first baseman for the Detroit Tigers, who came from the Deep South state of Georgia, said, "I wish Robinson all the luck in the world, and I hope he makes good."

Branch Rickey was determined to give him every chance. That's why he had decided to send Jackie to the Montreal Royals. Montreal was in Canada, which didn't have a history of slavery and segregation and prejudice. Most Canadians couldn't figure out what all the fuss was about. They just settled back to see what kind of a ballplayer this Jackie Robinson would turn out to be.

"I want you to run those bases like lightning. I want you to worry the daylights out of those pitchers," Branch Rickey had told him. "Don't be afraid to try stealing that extra base. I want you to be a daring player, one who isn't afraid to take a chance. Just go out there and run like the devil."

That's exactly what Jackie did, from the

very first day. And before long sportswriters were beginning to issue glowing accounts of the man who wasn't supposed to have the right stuff to play serious ball.

"There doesn't seem to be anything he can't do," marveled one writer. "His most obvious stock in trade is his noodle. I don't think there is a smarter player in the International League."

"Much of his popularity is due to the fact that Robbie is always coming up with something new," another stated.

"He bunts better than ninety percent of the big league players and runs better than seventy-five percent, even when it sounds like half the people in the stadium are yelling ugly things at him," a third added.

That was the trouble. The people of Montreal loved Jackie from the beginning. But only half of any baseball team's games are played at home. The rest of the time the Royals traveled from city to city, mostly in the United States. And there Jackie never knew what to expect. Sometimes he was cheered, but often he was heckled and booed.

Several pitchers made a habit of trying to

hit his head with fast balls traveling up to ninety miles per hour. They were trying to frighten him into playing bad ball. But it didn't work. As the manager of one of those teams admitted later, "I offered to buy a suit of clothes for any pitcher on our club who could knock him down. But he just brushed himself off and came back to play better than ever."

One day in Syracuse an opposing player pushed a mangy black cat out onto the field. "Hey, Jackie," he called, "there's your cousin clowning around out there!"

He hoped to make Jackie so angry he would lose his concentration. But Jackie answered this insult in his own special way. His next time at bat he slashed a double down the left field line. When the next Montreal player singled to center he dashed home from second base. As he crossed home plate, he grinned and called toward the Syracuse dugout, "I reckon my cousin's pretty happy now, huh?"

"That was Jackie," one of his teammates said. "The more mean things he was called, the tougher he got. . . ."

By the end of the season Jackie Robinson had become a true star. He led the International League in batting and fielding. He had also stolen forty bases and, as one Jackie-watcher put it, "the hearts of the fans of Montreal."

Jackie seemed to take both the good and the bad in easy stride. But his outer calm masked a tremendous inner tension. "I knew that every move I made was being watched and everything I did required the deepest concentration," he wrote later. "I knew that if I didn't succeed, nobody would try again for a long, long time."

By the end of the season he could barely eat or sleep. Finally he went to see a doctor. "Mr. Robinson, you are on the verge of a nervous breakdown," the doctor told him. "You must take at least ten days' rest. Don't read about baseball in the newspaper. Don't even listen to the game on the radio. You must do nothing but relax."

Jackie tried to follow the doctor's advice. "But I was worried about the team," he confessed. So he was back playing with the Royals only two days later.

Such devotion paid off. The Montreal Royals won first place in the International League. This meant they would face the Louisville Colonels of the American Association for the minor league championship.

The first three games of the series were played in Louisville, Kentucky, a completely segregated southern city. Usually, when Jackie played, many Negroes came to cheer on "the one," as they'd begun to call him. But now Louisville city officials decided to allow only a few Negroes into the ballpark. And they had to sit in a segregated section of the upper bleachers. So the stands were almost solidly white—and solidly hostile.

"I'd been insulted by experts," Jackie said. "But never anything like this." As he trotted onto the field, an explosion of boos rained down on him from the stands. "It was like being punched in the nose," a teammate recalled.

This rough treatment finally got through to Jackie. He still carried himself with what one writer called "effortless dignity." But he didn't play nearly as well as usual. Neither did the rest of the Royals. The Colonels easily won two out of the first three games. This meant that Louisville was a strong favorite to win the series as well.

Then the two teams moved north to Montreal for the rest of the games. The Montreal fans knew what kind of treatment their Jackie Robinson had just suffered. So now, when the Colonels trotted out onto *their* field, five thousand voices filled the air, booing them.

Jackie had to bite his lip to keep from smiling. It wasn't such a bad feeling to hear somebody else get booed for a change. Most of all it made him feel good to know that the people of Montreal cared so much about him.

This support also filled him with determination. He just couldn't let them down! Jackie found he was saying a prayer as the game began. He was praying for strength, for courage, for that extra something to turn this series around.

The Colonels took an early lead, however. The score was 5–4. But then in the ninth inning the Colonels' pitcher suddenly lost his control. A few minutes later the bases were loaded, with Jackie on third.

As the pitcher wound up to throw to the next batter, Jackie suddenly scampered off third and rushed headlong toward home plate. The crowd gasped with excitement. This was the kind of bold baseball they'd come to expect from Jackie Robinson. Then he skidded to a stop and raced back to third before the pitcher could pick him off.

For several moments the pitcher peered at him, frowning. Jackie was making him nervous. As he threw his next pitch, Jackie was off and headed for home once more. The catcher fumbled the ball and Jackie slid home with the tying run.

And that wasn't all. His next time at bat, he smashed a single to center field, which brought another Montreal runner across home plate. The game was over. And Montreal was back in the series.

Jackie kept right on playing daring baseball, and his fire fueled the rest of the team. As Montreal fans shouted and cheered, the Royals swept the next two games. They, with Jackie as their star, had snatched victory from what so recently looked like almost

certain defeat. They were the minor league champions of the world.

Oh, what a time everyone had after that last game! Thousands of fans rushed out of the stands to congratulate Jackie. Men slapped him on the back. Women hugged and kissed him. Children tugged at his clothes and begged for autographs.

Then several young men lifted Jackie onto their shoulders and paraded him around the field, laughing and cheering and singing *"Il a gagné ses épaulettes"*—"He has won his medals today."

Finally Jackie made his way to the locker room. There he met the manager of the Royals—the man who a few months before had asked Branch Rickey, "Do you think niggers are really human beings?" Now a grinning Clay Hopper was coming to shake hands. "Jackie, you're a great ballplayer and a fine gentleman," he said. "You're the greatest competitor I've ever seen. It's been wonderful having you on my team."

Well, well, Jackie thought. Maybe Mr. Rickey had been right. He had once said that prejudice was the world's biggest coward, and it always ran away in the face of fact.

When Jackie left the locker room, he found that hundreds of fans were still waiting for him. They just didn't want to let him go. For a few minutes he shook hands and signed autographs. Then he yelled out that he had a train to catch. And still the fans wouldn't get out of the way.

Finally Jackie did the only thing he could—he started to run down the street, and the crowd ran after him. Just then several of Jackie's friends drove by in a car. "Hop in!" one of them called. As Jackie tumbled into the backseat the driver turned and said, "Quite a day, huh?"

Jackie looked back at the crowd in the street. He'd been laughing. But now he grew serious. "Yes, quite a day," he said softly. "Quite a day."

A sportswriter who saw this amazing scene described it in his own way. "It was probably the only day in history that a black man ran from a white mob which had love instead of lynching on its mind," he wrote.

The Loneliest Man

A MAJOR BATTLE HAD INDEED BEEN WON. But the real war was only beginning. In the spring of 1947 Branch Rickey issued a press release. "Brooklyn announces the purchase of the contract of Jack Roosevelt Robinson from Montreal. He will report to the Dodgers immediately."

Rickey expected that the other Dodger players would be pleased by this news. They knew how well Jackie could play, after all. But some of them were still determined to keep baseball a white man's game.

They asked all the team members to sign a petition saying they would not play with Jackie. But Leo Durocher, the Dodgers' tough manager, soon put a stop to that. "Some guys here are causing trouble," he snapped. "Well, I don't care one bit how you feel. It doesn't mean a thing to me whether this guy Robinson is blue or orange or black or striped like a zebra! I manage this team.

And I say he plays. . . ."

That was the end of the petition. A few of the players, however, were so unhappy that they asked Branch Rickey to trade them to another team. One was the great outfielder Dixie Walker. "I'd rather stay home and paint my house than play with that guy," he said. Another was a young catcher named Bobby Bragan. "Mr. Rickey," he said, "I live down in Forth Worth, Texas. My friends there would never forgive me."

Branch Rickey listened to them. He didn't get angry, for he understood that they were being asked to do something they'd been told all their lives was wrong. But he also held firm. He told them he would trade them later in the season if they still felt the same way. But they must understand one thing very clearly. Jackie Robinson was in the major leagues, and he was there to stay.

April fifteenth was the opening day of the 1947 season. And Jackie Robinson, with the number 42 on the back of his uniform, took his place at first base at Ebbets Field in Brooklyn.

Jackie scanned the audience until he

found the one person he was looking for. He'd been married for more than a year. Now he flashed a brief smile at his wife, Rae, who was sitting in the stands with their baby, Jackie, Jr., in her arms. Then he turned and began to play ball.

At first most of the Dodgers were extremely cool to Jackie. Some would nod and say hello. But nobody really talked to him in the locker room. When he sat down in the dugout, players like Dixie Walker and Bobby Bragan made it a point to get up and sit somewhere else. And Eddie Stanky even walked up to him and said, "You're on this ball club, and as far as I'm concerned, that makes you one of twenty-five players on my team. But I want you to know I don't like it. I want you to know I don't like you." That summed up the general feeling of the team. As one sportswriter put it, "I'd say he's the loneliest man in baseball."

This treatment was mild compared to what he had to face from some of the opposing teams. Late in April the Philadelphia Phillies came to Brooklyn to play a three-

game series. Ben Chapman, the team's manager, had a real hatred of blacks. He ordered his players to challenge Jackie with every kind of racial insult they could think of "to see if he can take it."

It began when Jackie first came up to bat.

"Hey, burr-head, why aren't you out picking cotton where you belong?"

"Yeah, coon, do you always smell so bad?"

"Hey, shoeshine boy, come shine my shoes!"

"They're waiting for you in the jungles, black boy. So why don't you go back there? We sure don't want you here!"

Later Jackie would admit that this day brought him closer to cracking up than he'd ever been before. He knew he should be used to this kind of treatment by now. But he wasn't. He found himself trembling as tortured questions tumbled through his mind. What did Mr. Rickey expect of him? He was, after all, a human being. How could either of them have thought that the barriers would fall? That his talent could triumph over such hate?

Suddenly he was filled with a hot feeling close to sickness. He wrote later that for one wild rage-crazed minute he was ready to give up on Mr. Rickey's "noble experiment." "It isn't going to work. I've made every effort to work hard, to get myself in shape. My best is not enough for them."

More than anything he wanted to throw down his bat, stride over to the Phillies dugout, grab one of those players, and smash his teeth in with his despised black fist. Then he would walk away from baseball forever.

Then Jackie thought about Branch Rickey. He remembered how Mr. Rickey had not listened when his family and friends and colleagues had all begged him not to fight to make Jackie the first black player in professional baseball. "Mr. Rickey had come to a moral crossroads and made a lonely decision," Jackie wrote later. "Well, I was at a crossroads, too. And I would make mine. I would stay, no matter what." This was the most difficult decision he'd ever made.

Another Dodger remembered that day. "At no time in my life," he said, "have I heard racial poison to match the abuse that

Ben Chapman and some of his players sprayed on Robinson during that game. They mentioned everything from a Negro's supposedly extra-thick skull to the repulsive sores and diseases the rest of us would get if we touched the towels he used."

Somehow Jackie found the strength to hold on. Then at last, during the third game, something changed. Eddie Stanky—the same man who had so recently told Jackie he didn't want him on the team—suddenly came to Jackie's defense.

"Listen, you yellow-bellied cowards," he screamed into the Philadelphia dugout, "what kind of men are you, anyway? Why . . . don't you pick on someone who can fight back? You know Robinson can't!"

Later Branch Rickey said that he had been sickened by the Phillies' racial attacks. But in the end it had been good for the Dodgers. For this abuse, more than anything else, started to "solidify and unite the entire team behind Jackie. Not one of them was willing to sit by and see someone kick around a man who had his hands tied behind his back."

Oh, What a Year!

JACKIE WAS GOING TO BE UNDER TREMEN-
dous pressure for the rest of the season.
Red Barber, a radio broadcaster known as
the "Voice of the Brooklyn Dodgers," put it
this way: "This business of being the first
was not something you were confronted with
one day and then didn't have to worry about
anymore. It had to be handled inning by inning, game by game, day by day. It was
there all the time because when Jackie Robinson came, he came to stay."

On the field opposing fans and players
continued to boo and taunt him. Off the
field things were rough, too. Many times
when on the road, Jackie couldn't stay with
the team at a hotel. Often he'd have to eat
alone in his room or at some Negro-only restaurant. Almost every day he received hate
letters and calls from people who threatened
to hurt his wife, kidnap his child, and even
kill him if he didn't quit the game.

Jackie said that this never-ending pressure might have proved too much for him except for one thing—the people who stood by him through it all.

One was his wife, of course. "I didn't miss a game," Rae remembered. "It was like going to work with your husband. I held on to Jack. He held on to me."

Another was Branch Rickey. "He was like a father to me," Jackie wrote. "The father I never had."

And then there was a very special friend. Pee Wee Reese, a man many called "the Kentucky Colonel," played shortstop for the Dodgers. Right from the beginning he was more than just another teammate. He was someone who truly understood what Jackie was going through.

When Pee Wee had been asked to sign the petition against Jackie, he refused. "I've thought about this thing a great deal," he said. "And I ended up putting myself in Robinson's place. I said to myself, suppose Negroes were in the majority in this country and for years baseball had been closed to white players. Then somebody gave *me* a chance to be the first white player on a Negro team. Well, I'd be awfully . . . scared and lonesome and I sure would appreciate the guy who didn't go out of his way to give me a kick in the teeth."

Pee Wee was the first Dodger to insist that Jackie join the others in a card game. When things got tense, he tried to make Jackie relax with some little joke. And one day, early in the season, he showed a very hostile audience just where he stood about all this race business. For several innings people in the stands had been shouting the usual insults at Jackie. Then they started in on Pee Wee, as well. Reese was one of the most popular men in baseball. These fans, however, thought of him as a traitor—a man from the South who played on the same team as Jackie Robinson.

They shouted things like "How can you stand there next to that nigger?" And "Hey, Kentucky boy! When your grandpappy finds out how you been socializing and fraternizing with colored folks, he's gonna turn over in his grave!"

For a while Pee Wee just ignored it all.

68

But suddenly, as the calls got louder, he strode over to Jackie and put an arm around his shoulder. The two men talked quietly for a minute or two. Then Pee Wee walked back to his position. He had shown the world that he was proud to be playing with Jackie Robinson.

More and more Americans were beginning to share this pride in Jackie. People who had never thought about blacks began to root for this underdog. Many others, who had believed all their lives that Negroes were inferior, began to admire his aggressive playing style and his dignity under pressure.

There were two groups of fans that pleased Jackie particularly. First, the young white children who came to cheer him on so wildly. Jackie felt this hero worship was very important. "Maybe because of it they'll grow up to be less prejudiced," he said.

The other group of fans that were especially dear to Jackie Robinson were blacks. Wherever he played, huge crowds turned out. "You've never seen anything like it," a sportswriter remembered. "People in wheelchairs came. Little old grandmothers in their nineties came. *Everyone* came. Often they traveled hundreds of miles on special trains and buses to see him in action. Lots of times they'd stay even after those buses and trains had left. They wanted to see Robinson field one more ball, steal one more base, hit one more time."

For Jackie was giving black Americans perhaps the most important thing of all. Hope. One Negro who grew up to play in the major leagues remembered that time when life in too many places was so hard for black people. "And then Jackie came and it was like, 'My dreams have come true. Now we'll have that opportunity to prove to the world that given a fair chance, we can produce.' "

Through all the booing and all the cheering Jackie played spectacular baseball. Sportswriters called him "the Technicolor Terror," "the Black Meteor," and said that "he burned with a dark fire."

"Jackie could do anything. He could hit and bunt and steal and run."

"He brought a new dimension into baseball. He dances and prances off base, keeping the enemy infield off balance and worrying the pitcher to death."

"There were times when I thought he was the team. All the skills and speed that made it possible for him to excel in basketball, football, track and field were set in motion on whatever field he was on."

And "Jackie Robinson was the most exciting player I have ever seen. As long as he was in the game, you had a chance to win. The second he got on base, the whole ballpark got on the edge of their seats. They knew he was going to do something. It was just a matter of time. He played baseball with such abandon. He did things."

Toward the end of the season it became clear that the Dodgers were going to win the pennant for the first time in six years.

When the team got back to New York from their last western tour, more than three thousand wildly cheering fans met their train. As it rolled into Pennsylvania Station, a band struck up and the happy throng began to yell, "There's Dixie!" and "Stankey!" and "Pee Wee!"

Then Jackie stepped off the train. Instantly he was mobbed. Fans pounded him on the back and shook his hand until it was so numb he couldn't feel his fingers. Finally six policemen cleared a path through the crush and escorted him to the subway that would take him home to his family.

The fans continued to chase after him. Almost fifty of them, laughing and singing, "Hail, Hail, the Gang's All Here," and shouting "We've done it!" and "Jackie's our man!" piled into the subway car with him. As Jackie said later, "That was *some* ride!"

A few days later Jackie was named Rookie of the Year by *Sporting News*, the magazine that just two years before had said, "There's not a single Negro player with major league possibilities."

Dodger fans honored him at a special Jackie Robinson Day at Ebbets Field. In the ceremonies at home plate Jackie was given a number of gifts, including a gold watch, a TV set, and a Cadillac. But he knew the most important gift he had received that season was something he couldn't see. It was the respect and affection of so many of his fellow Dodgers.

There was Pee Wee, of course. "He [Robinson] has more than proved himself in every way," the little shortstop from Kentucky said simply.

And Duke Snider, who later wrote, "I grew to admire and respect him as a person even more than as an athlete that season. What he had to go through as the first black player was unbelievable. But he stuck it out and developed into the greatest competitor I've ever seen."

What pleased Jackie most of all were the changed opinions of some of the people who hadn't wanted him there at all. People like Dixie Walker, who announced that "I want to be the first to say it. No other ballplayer on this club has done more to put the Dodgers up in the race than Robinson has. He is everything Branch Rickey said he was."

Bobby Bragan said, "Being Jackie Robinson's teammate was one of the best breaks I ever got. Watching what he had to go through helped make me a better, more enlightened man."

Jackie Speaks Out

IN ONE SHORT SEASON JACKIE HAD PROVED that Negroes could not only compete in the major leagues—they could, as one person put it, "sparkle." In the next few years the Dodgers and other teams would be enriched by such black players as Roy Campanella, Don Newcombe, Monte Irvin, Junior Gilliam, Larry Doby, and Hank Thompson. And it was all made possible for them, as one newspaperman wrote, because "of the dignity and skill and intelligence of Jack Roosevelt Robinson."

Right before the 1949 season, Branch Rickey sent for Jackie. "I told him that the noble experiment had been a complete success, and that he had come through with courage far beyond what I had asked. But I knew how hard it had been for him not to fight back, how the tensions had built up in him. So now he could be on his own. From now on he could do anything he felt like doing."

Oh, how good it felt—not having to turn that other cheek anymore! Soon after, one of his teammates was at bat when the umpire looked at a ball and called it a strike. The Dodger players knew it was a bad decision. They started to protest loudly. The umpire warned them to stop. But Jackie and a few others continued the heckling. Finally the umpire whirled around and pointed, "You! Robinson. You're out of the game!"

Jackie felt great as he trotted off the field. He'd been treated exactly like any other ballplayer who happened to get on an umpire's nerves. One of the newspapers said it all in what Jackie thought was the best headline he'd ever read about himself: JACKIE JUST ANOTHER GUY.

Some time later he and Pee Wee were warming up before a game. Pee Wee happened to make an especially hard throw that hit Jackie's glove with a loud *thwack*. "Yow!" Jackie yelled, shaking his hand.

An opposing player was standing nearby. Jackie remembered this man all too well, for he had been a Philadelphia Phillie in the days when Jackie couldn't talk back. And he had taunted him with some of the most vicious racial slurs Jackie had ever heard.

Now the man said in a mocking voice, "Be careful, Pee Wee. Don't throw so hard, or you'll hurt *Mr.* Robinson's hand."

Pee Wee said afterward that as long as he lived, he'd never forget what happened next. "Robinson strolled over and pushed his chin right into the man's face and barked, 'Listen . . . I haven't forgotten those days in 1947 when you called me some unprintable filthy names, and I couldn't talk back. Well, I *can* talk back now, and I just want to tell you that if you say one more word *to* me or *about* me, I'll . . .'" Jackie told him off in no uncertain terms.

"I tell you the truth," Pee Wee added. "I felt good right down to my toenails to see that, years later, this guy finally got what was coming to him. When Robinson challenged him, he shriveled up like a snail, and we never heard another peep out of him."

From now on Jackie would say whatever he wanted to as a ballplayer. He would also express himself freely about being black in a

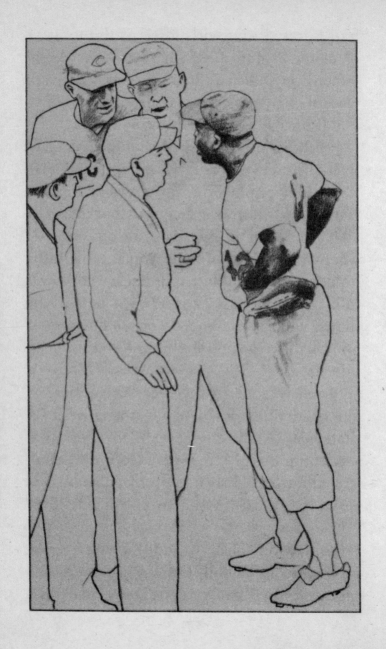

segregated America, and that got him into a lot of trouble. For this was the late 1940s and early 1950s—before a young minister named Martin Luther King, Jr., had started the Civil Rights Movement.

Back then, blacks were supposed to be grateful for whatever they had, no matter how little it was. But Jackie wanted equal opportunity for all blacks in all walks of life. And he spoke out about it.

"I'm grateful for all the breaks and honors and opportunities I've had, but I always believe I won't have it made until the humblest black kid in the most remote backwoods of America has it made," Jackie said.

And "If I had a room jammed with trophies and awards, and a child of mine came to me and asked what I had done in defense of black people and decent whites fighting for freedom, and I had to tell that child I had kept quiet, that I had been timid, I would have to mark myself a total failure in the whole business of living."

And "I have to speak out because deep in my heart I know that no Negro, however famous, however great his contributions, is safe from the poison darts of racial bigotry. Crowds can cheer him, clubs can heap their choicest honors on him, but as long as *any* Negro is unfree, *every* Negro is unfree—for in the minds of millions the most accomplished black man will remain 'just another Negro.' "

This kind of talk upset many people. Some began to call Jackie names such as "troublemaker" and "pop-off." Jackie wrote, "I learned that as long as I appeared to ignore insult and injury, I was a hero to a lot of people who had sympathy for the underdog. But the minute I began to sound off, I became a swell-head, a wise guy, an 'uppity' nigger." He wrote, "It is a sad truth that the closer the Negro gets to first-class citizenship, the fewer his supporters are. . . ."

He also wrote that he was "the kind of Negro who's come to the conclusion that he isn't going to beg for anything, that he will be reasonable but he . . . is tired of being patient. And if that makes some people uncomfortable, that's tough."

That was Jackie Robinson, a tough-spirited man off the field as well as on.

For the next few years Jackie was the sensation of baseball. He was awesome at bat, a wizard in the field, and a plain terror on the bases, as one sportswriter said. Often he led the league in batting, stolen bases, and runs batted in. Before his playing days were over, he would help power the Dodgers to six pennants and one World Series Championship.

Statistics could never really tell why Jackie Robinson was considered such a great ballplayer. It was his fierce spirit that earned him the title "the most dangerous man in baseball."

"Robbie was the difference, the squeezer," a teammate remembered. "The fellow who twisted the screws on the pressure cooker that cooked the other team's goose. He was the only player I ever saw who could completely turn a game around by himself."

"The thing about Jackie," a rival player commented, "was that he could find more ways to beat you. He was always up to something." Jackie proved this again and again. But the game sportswriters would always remember best was the last one of the 1951 season.

The Dodgers were tied for first place, but they had to win this game against the Philadelphia Phillies to be National League Champions.

In the ninth inning the score was tied, and the game went into extra innings. In the twelfth, Don Newcombe, the Dodger pitcher, weakened, and the Phillies loaded the bases. The next Phillie came to bat. Newcombe pitched. The batter swung and cracked a line drive toward right center field. If it got there the game—and the Dodgers' dreams of a pennant—were over.

But Jackie flung himself, from his position at second base, into a full-length power dive and somehow managed to get his glove on the ball. It was, as a fan said, "one of the most incredibly sensational catches in the history of baseball."

Jackie was completely off-balance, though. He crashed face down to the ground. As he hit, his right elbow rammed into his stomach. It felt like being hit by a sledge hammer, he said later. For a moment he blacked out. Then a terrible pain spread through his chest. It was so bad he could barely take a breath.

Somehow Jackie continued to play during the next inning. But the pain didn't go away. It got worse and worse. All his strength seemed to be gone. His legs felt too weak to hold him up, and he was sick to his stomach. Finally, in the fourteenth inning, with the score still tied, he decided he had to ask for a replacement, a pinch-hitter.

He didn't, though. Suddenly it was his turn at bat, and he found himself standing at home plate. The pitcher broke a curve over the inside corner . . .

And from somewhere inside himself Jackie found the strength to come back. He swung . . . A deafening roar came from the crowd. Jackie had hit a home run over the left field fence. The Dodgers had won!

No wonder people said he was one of the greatest clutch players of all time. He always came through when the going got tough.

By the mid-fifties Jackie was slowing down. He was over thirty now. His hair was turning gray. He'd gained some weight. The spring was gone from his legs. One writer dubbed him "an old gray fat man."

Yet when he played, there was still that special sense of excitement, that feeling that anything could happen. It did in the first game of the 1955 World Series. Brooklyn was playing the Yankees. It was the eighth inning, with Jackie at bat. He took a ball and a strike. Then he slammed a grounder to left field. Running with a rare burst of speed, he made it to second. When another batter flied out, Jackie advanced to third.

The next Dodger came to bat, and Jackie took off from third base. As in the early days he danced. He pranced. He worried the Yankee pitcher. But from the Yankee dugout a voice called, "Don't worry about Robinson! He's too slow to go anywhere!"

The pitcher thought so, too. He concentrated on the batter—and Jackie took off once more. He meant it this time. The pitcher threw frantically to home plate, but Jackie slid in ahead of the tag. He had stolen home.

"How's that for an old gray fat man?" he called out gleefully as he picked himself up.

The End Came Too Soon

I'M LOOKING FORWARD TO SPENDING more time with my family," thirty-six-year-old Jackie said as he retired at the end of the 1956 season. He and Rae had three children now—Jackie, Jr., Sharon, and David.

Jackie began to fill his life with many different activities. He became vice-president of Chock Full O' Nuts, a chain of restaurants. He wrote a newspaper column and was the author of several books, including two autobiographies. He also worked for many minority causes.

He became director of the National Association for the Advancement of Colored People. When he received this organization's highest honor, the Spingarn Medal, he announced, "To be honored in this way by the NAACP means more than anything that has happened to me before. That is because the NAACP . . . represents everything that a man should stand for: human dignity, brotherhood, fair play . . ."

Jackie spearheaded a lengthy tour across the country for the National Conference of Christians and Jews, seeking to arouse a deeper concern for the basic brotherhood of *all* people—blacks and whites, Christians and Jews.

But perhaps Jackie was most deeply concerned about the black youngsters growing up in urban slums—children whose lives were being twisted by the poverty and frustration they were forced to live with. So he gave a great deal of time to the Harlem YMCA, where he tried to teach children, as he said, "about self-respect, the meaning of ambition, and a hope for the future."

He marched at the side of Martin Luther King, Jr., through the civil rights years. And he participated in politics, supporting people who were willing to fight for blacks.

Then it was the year 1972. Jackie Robinson was only fifty-three. But he had been battling diabetes and heart trouble for years. Now he was almost blind. He didn't let this stop him. In October of 1972—twenty-five years after he had broken the color barrier in baseball—Jackie attended the World Series in Cincinnati. A fan came up to him and held out a baseball. "Would you autograph it for me?" he asked.

"I'm sorry," Jackie apologized. "I can't see it. If I wrote anything, I'd be sure to mess up the other names you have on it."

The fan kept on holding out the ball. "There are no other names, Mr. Robinson," he said quietly. "The only one I want is yours." Jackie signed the ball.

Nine days later, on October 24, Jackie Robinson was dead. Twenty-five hundred people crowded the Riverside Church in New York for his funeral. Many more stood outside. The Reverend Jesse Jackson delivered the eulogy. He spoke of how a body may die, but how the deeds of a man live on. "When Jackie took the field, something reminded us of our birthright to be free. . . . We are all better because a man with a mission passed our way."

Others tried to express how they felt about Jack Roosevelt Robinson.

His friend Pee Wee Reese: "I know I

couldn't have done what Jackie did. But Jackie was tough. He could take care of himself."

His brother Mack: "He broke the color line in baseball. But he created a social revolution that went much farther than that. Blacks have made it in all areas because Jackie Robinson showed the world we could."

Fellow Dodger Gil Hodges: "For sheer courage, I would pick Jackie anytime. He just never backed up."

The sportswriter Red Smith: "He simply would not be defeated. Not by the other team and not by life."

Jackie always believed that a life was not important except in the ways it affected other lives. So perhaps another of Jackie's close friends, the writer Roger Kahn, said best what everyone was struggling to express. "If his death has robbed my wife, my children, and me of an admired friend, we are still fortunate for having had the friendship of Jackie Robinson. . . . So is all the family of man."

1919 On January 31 Jack Roosevelt Robinson, the fifth and youngest child of Mallie and Jerry Robinson, is born in rural Georgia.

1920 The Robinson household moves to California.

1933 At Muir Technical High School Jackie becomes a baseball, football, basketball, and track star.

1937 Jackie enters Pasadena Junior College.

1938 In May Jackie competes in two important sports events held on the same day in two towns more than forty miles apart. He sets a new junior college world record in the broad jump. Then he helps his baseball team become junior college champions.

1939 Jackie is offered a sports scholarship to attend the University of California at Los Angeles.

1942 World War II is raging, and Jackie, a private in the U.S. Army, is sent to Fort Riley, Kansas.

1943 In January, after a battle with a widespread policy that says "Negroes are not leaders of men," Jackie graduates from Officers Candidate School as a lieutenant.

1944 In November Jackie is discharged from the army.

1945 In April he becomes a ballplayer with the Kansas City Monarchs, an all-Negro baseball team.

On October 23 a short statement is released to the press, saying that Jackie Robinson has been signed to play the 1946 season with the Montreal Royals.

1946 On February 10 Jackie and Rachel Isum are married.

In September, with Jackie sparking the team, the Montreal Royals win the Little World Series and become minor league champions of the world.

1947 On April 15, the opening day of the 1947 season, Jackie Robinson, with the number 42 on his back, takes his place has a major league ballplayer on Ebbets Field in Brooklyn, New York.

On September 12 Jackie is named "Rookie of the Year."

On September 23 thousands of fans pay tribute to him at a special Jackie Robinson Day at Ebbets Field.

1956 At the end of the season thirty-six-year-old Jackie Robinson retires from baseball and participates in many business and humanitarian activities.

1962 Jackie becomes the first Negro to be inducted into baseball's Hall of Fame.

1972 In June Jackie attends the twenty-fifth anniversary of his major league debut at Dodger Stadium in Los Angeles, California, where the club honors him by retiring his number 42.

On October 24, Jackie Robinson dies.